BEGINNING
SIGN
LANGUAGE
SERIES

Expanded

Songs in Sign

by S. Harold Collins

Illustrated by Kathy Kifer, Jane Schneider, Dahna Solar and Marina Krasnik

Expanded Songs in Sign presents familiar songs fully illustrated in Signed English. These are songs that will encourage beginning signers and develop their facility for signing.

Music and signs are presented for eleven songs:

If You're Happy 3

Twinkle, Twinkle Little Star 6

Bingo 8

Row, Row, Row Your Boat 10

The Muffin Man 12

The Mulberry Bush 14

London Bridge 17

Over the River & Through the Woods 20

Tell Me Why 24

She'll Be Coming 'Round the Mountain . . . 26

The Bear Went Over the Mountain 28

Special thanks to: Jeff Corbett, Amanda Corbett, Arias Solar, Elena Collins, Emily Collins, Carissa Albin, Colleen Kerns, Austin Griffith, Ariel Solar, Paul Albin.

Published by
Garlic Press
605 Powers St.
Eugene, OR 97402

ISBN 978-0-931993-05-9
Order No. GP-005

www.garlicpress.com
Printed in China

If You're Happy

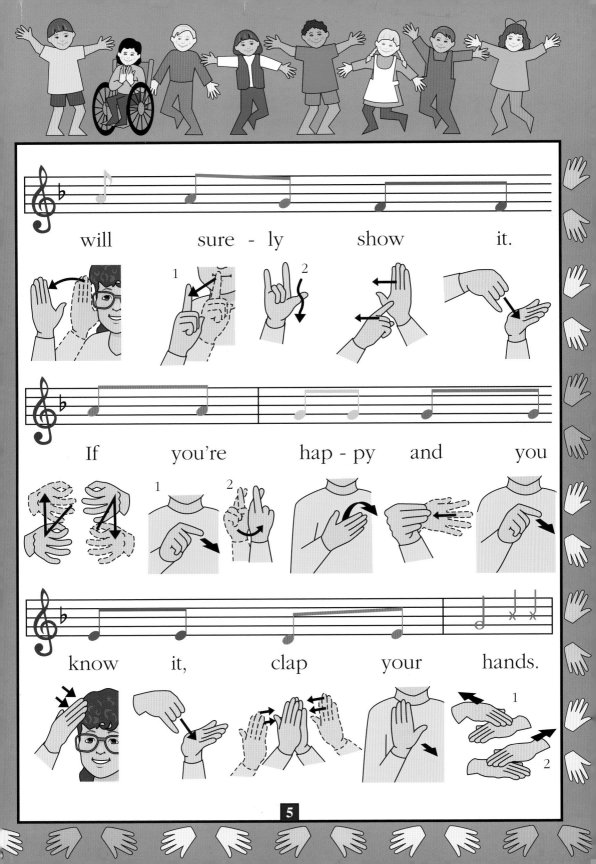

Twinkle, Twinkle, Little Star

Twin-kle, twin-kle, lit - tle star

How I won-der what you are!

Up a - bove the world so high,

Bingo

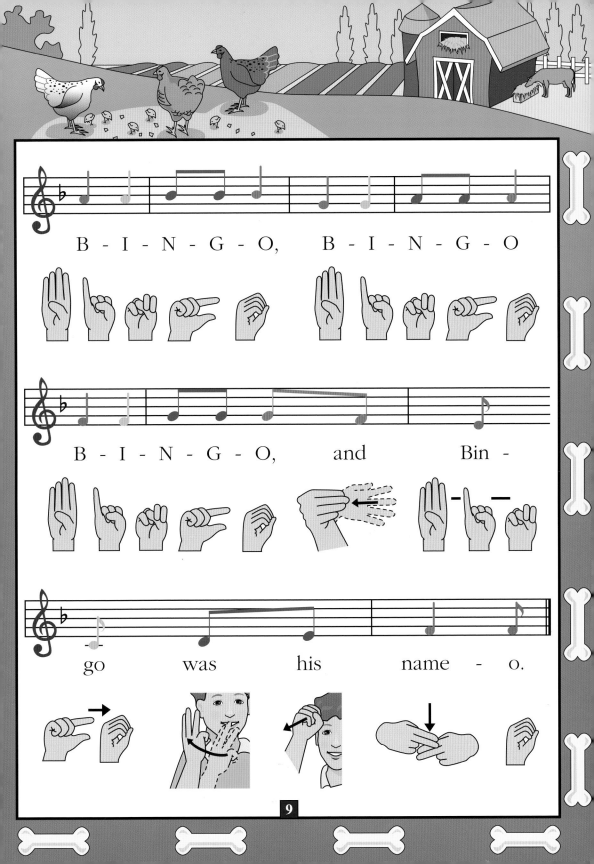

Row, Row, Row Your Boat

The Muffin Man

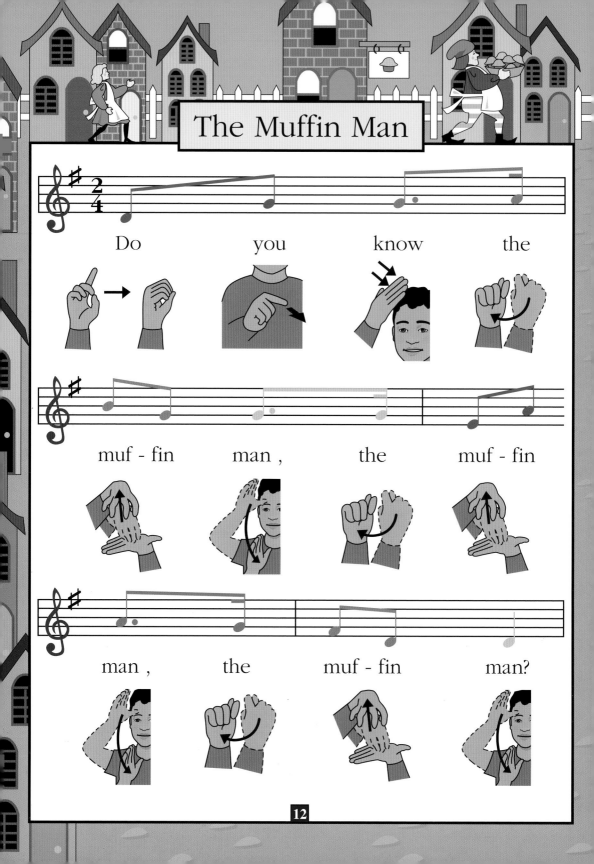

The Mulberry Bush

1. Here we go 'round

the mul-ber-ry bush, the mul-ber-ry

bush, the mul-ber-ry bush.

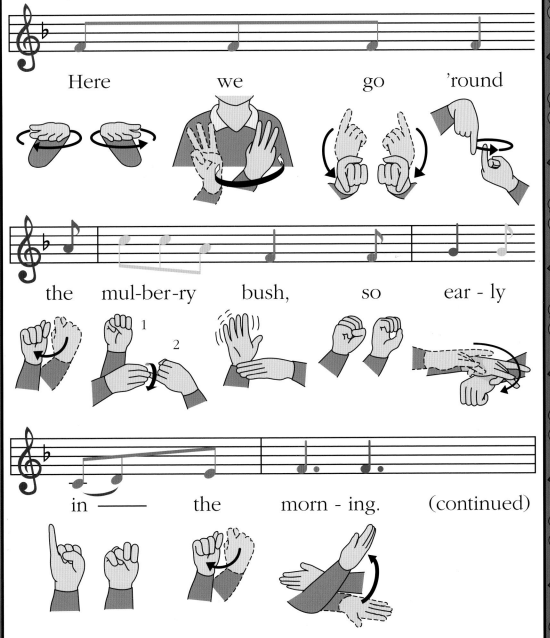

Here   we   go   'round

the   mul-ber-ry   bush,   so   ear - ly

in ——— the   morn - ing.   (continued)

2. This   is   the   way   we

wash   our   face,   (repeat)

3rd verse . . comb   our   hair,   (repeat)

4th verse . . brush   our   teeth, (repeat)

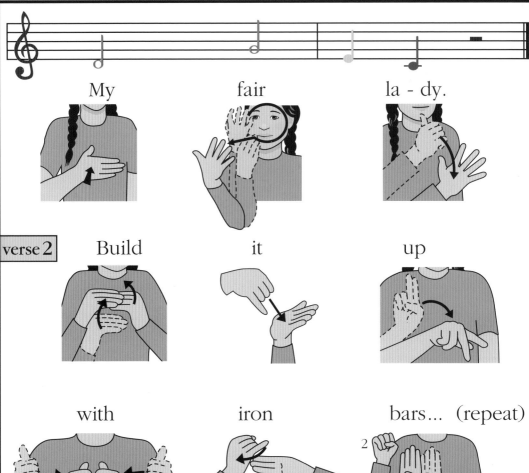

My fair la - dy.

verse 2

Build it up

with iron bars... (repeat)

18

Build   it   up   with

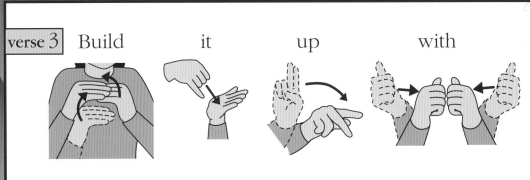

sticks   and   stones... (repeat)

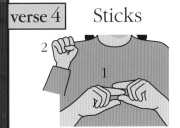

Sticks   and   stones   will

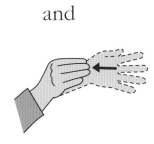

bend   and   break.... (repeat)

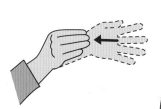

Over the River and Through the Woods

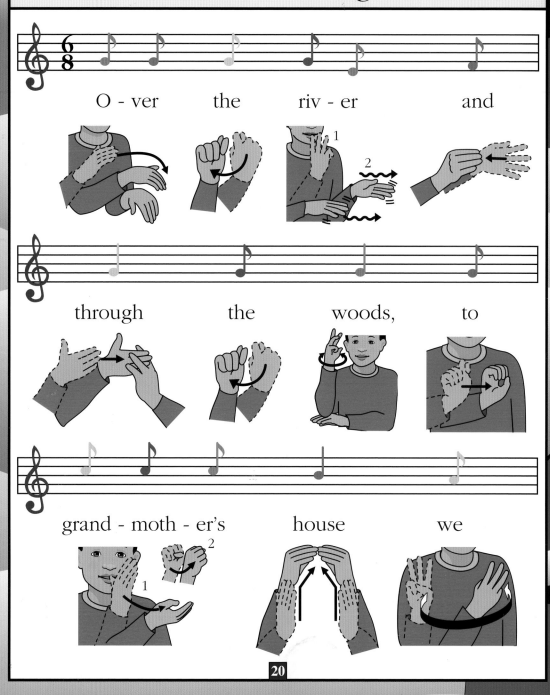

O - ver   the   riv - er   and

through   the   woods,   to

grand - moth - er's   house   we

Tell Me Why

tell ___ me why ___ the sky

is blue, And I will

tell you why I ___ love you.

1. She'll be com - ing 'round the

moun - tain when she comes.

She'll be coming 'round the mountain when she comes.

She'll be coming 'round the moun - tain,

She'll be coming 'round the moun - tain,

She'll be coming 'round the mountain when she comes.

2. She'll be driving six white

horses when she comes (repeat)

3. (She'll be) shining just like silver...

4. We will all go out to meet her...

The Bear Went Over the Mountain

The   bear   went

o - ver   the   moun - tain,

The   bear   went   o - ver   the   moun - tain,

The   bear   went   o - ver   the   moun - tain,

To see what

he could see. ———

To see what he could see, ———

To see what he could see ———

29

The   oth - er   side

of   the   moun - tain,

The oth - er side of the moun - tain,

The oth - er side of the moun - tain